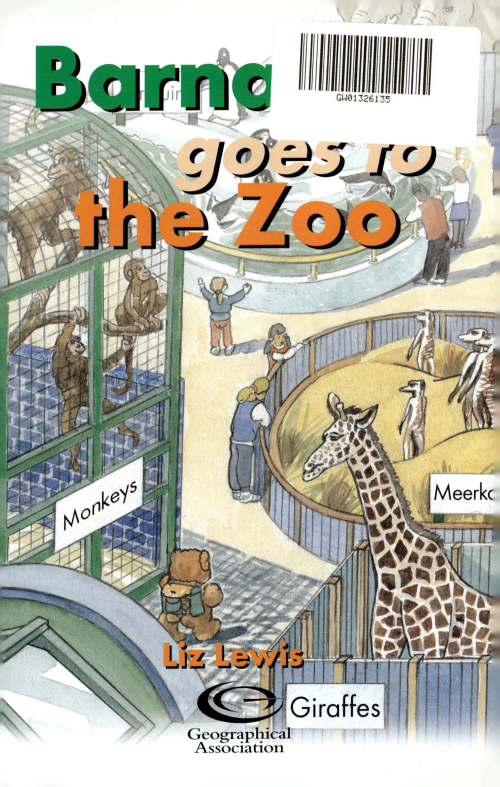

Barna

goes to the Zoo

Monkeys

Meerk

Liz Lewis

Giraffes

Geographical
Association

Barnaby Bear is visiting Dublin Zoo.
He has a map to help him find all
the animals.

Barnaby finds the big cats.
He sees a big stripy tiger.

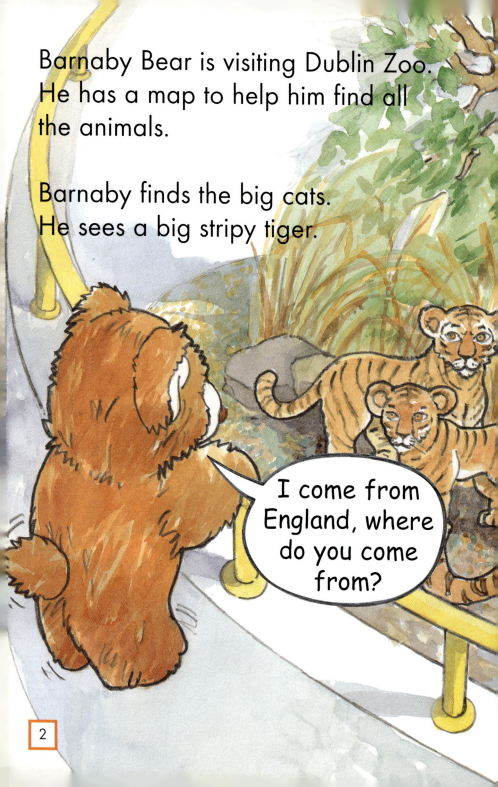

I come from England, where do you come from?

3

Barnaby sees a sleek, spotty cheetah.

I come from England, where do you come from?

Cheetahs like me live in the hot plains of Africa. We can run faster than anything else.

Barnaby finds the birds. He sees a pretty pink and white cockatoo.

I come from England, where do you come from?

Cockatoos like me live on islands in the warm China Sea. We love to eat coconuts.

Barnaby looks for the reptiles.
He finds a huge crocodile.

I come from England, where do you come from?

The crocodile opens his huge jaws and shows Barnaby his sharp teeth.

Crocodiles like me live in rivers and swamps in hot countries. My family comes from Australia.

Barnaby looks for the lion, the king of the jungle. But the lion sees him first!

HELLO LITTLE BEAR! WHERE DO YOU COME FROM?

Barnaby decides not to ask any more questions. Would you?

Thankyou for visiting
Dublin Zoo
please call again